bush theatre

The Bush Theatre
presents the world premiere of

Like a Fishbone

by Anthony Weigh

7 June – 10 July 2010

aka Westfield LONDON west 12 STAGE ELECTRICS

The Bush Theatre would like to give particular thanks to:
aka, West 12 Shopping Centre and Westfield London;
Alex Sherratt at Matthew Lloyd Architects, Robert Danton-Rees at Capital Models,
Haworth Tompkins Architects, Benet Brandreth, Flower Fayre
and Rebel Rebel for floral design

Like a Fishbone

by Anthony Weigh

Cast

The Architect	Deborah Findlay
The Mother	Sarah Smart
The Intern	Phoebe Waller-Bridge
The Child	Hannah Green
	Chloe Turner

Creative Team

Director	Josie Rourke
Designer	Lucy Osborne
Lighting Designer	James Farncombe
Sound Designer	Emma Laxton
Assistant Director	Simon Evans
Dialect Coach	William Conacher
Fight Director	Bret Yount
Company Stage Manager (*on the book*)	Mary Hely
Assistant Stage Manager	Jessica Harwood
Assistant Stage Manager (*placement*)	Ria O'Brien
Design Assistant	Joe Schermoly
Costume Supervisor	Liz Evans
Model Maker	Rachel Wingate

Company

Deborah Findlay (The Architect)

Theatre for the Bush includes: *Keyboard Skills, Commitments.*

Other theatre includes;*Separate Tables* (Chichester Festival Theatre); *Madame De Sade, John Gabriel Borkman,The Cut, The Vortex* (Donmar Warehouse); *The House of Bernarda, Alba,The Mandate, Mother Claps Molly House,The Winter's Tale, Once In A While* (National Theatre);*The Threesome, Cinderella And Her Sisters* (Lyric, Hammersmith); *Vincent River* (59e59 Theater, New York);*The School For Scandal, Merchant Of Venice, Twelfth Night, The New Inn, Three Sisters* (RSC);*The Crucible, Child's Play* (Crucible, Sheffield);*Tongue Of A Bird, Hedda Gabler* (Almeida);*The Overgrown Path, Tom And Viv* (Royal Court); *Top Girls* (Royal Court/New York); *Artists And Admirers* (Riverside Studios); *As You Like It, King Lear* (Oxford Stage Company); *Macbeth* (Nuffield, Southampton); *Stanley* (National Theatre / Circle In The Sq. NY);*The Seagull* (Thelma Holt / Tour); *The New Menosa* (The Gate Theatre); *The Clandestine Marriage* (Thelma Holt / West End); *The House of Bernada Alba* (West End); *The Beaux Stratagem* (Tour / Richmond).

Television includes: *Poirot, Silent Witness, Torchwood, Gunrush, Lewis, Cranford, Thin Ice, The Family Man, Foyle's War, State Of Play, Saving Grace, Anna Karenina,Midsomer Murders, Wives And Daughters, Heat Of The Sun, Kavanagh QC, Jane Eyre, Sherlock Holmes, Maigret, Natural Lies, Anglo Saxon Attitudes, House Of Bernarda Alba, Top Girls, First And Last, What If It's Raining.*

Film includes: *Summer, Vanity Fair, Me Without You, The End Of The Affair, Jack And Sarah, Truly Madly Deeply.*

Hannah Green (The Child)

Theatre includes: *High School Musical 2, The King and I* and *Showstoppers* (Kenneth More Theatre). Hannah is a member of The Academy Agency.

Other credits include: 'H&M' commercial directed by Johan Renck, the short film *Super Mommie, Super Heroine*, an internet viral for Bottica.com and a photographic campaign and live event for Barnardo's.

Phoebe Waller-Bridge (The Intern)

Theatre for the Bush includes: *2nd May 1997.*

Other theatre includes: *Rope* (Almedia and Sonia Friedman); *Roaring Trade* (Soho Theatre); *Twelfth Night* (Sprite Productions); *Crazy Love* (Paines Plough); *Is Everyone OK?* (Latitude Festival).

Television includes: *Doctors.*

Film includes: *The Reward.*

Phoebe is the Co-Artistic Director of DryWrite.

Sarah Smart (The Mother)

Theatre includes: *The Line* (Arcola); *Ghosts* (The Gate Theatre).

Television includes: *Wallander (Series 1 & 2), Identity, Casualty 1909, Miss Marple, Poirot, City Of Vice, Billy Goats Gruff, Whistleblowers, Yellow House, Five Days, Funland, Murder Prevention, Jane Hall, Love Again, Sparkhouse, At Home With The Braithwaites* (4 series), *Safe House, Sweet Revenge, Dalziel and Pascoe, The Bill, Soldier, Bliss (1& 2 Series), The Locksmith, A Touch Of Frost, Chase The Fade, Woof.*

TV Film includes: *David Copperfield, Wuthering Heights, Deadly Summer, Ball Trap On The Cote Sauvage.*

Radio includes: *Blood Wedding, Safety Catch, Martha's Metamorphosis, Madame Bovary, Strike, Miscreant Mothers, The Living And The Dead, The Provoked Wife, Another Big Day, The Beehive, Shubbery, Skullduggery.*

Chloe Turner (The Child)

Theatre includes: *Snow White and the Seven Dwarfs, Chas and Dave* (Thameside Theatre); *Rhythm* (Towngate Theatre).

Chloe is a member of Performers Agency in Essex

She recently appeared at the O2 Arena 'Voice in a Million' charity event as a vocalist.

Simon Evans (Assistant Director)

Simon has a BA in English and Drama with Education from Cambridge University.

Theatre as Director includes *Devolution* (Theatre 503/RRE); *Madness in Valencia* (Trafalgar Studios); *Firefly Heartbeat* (Tristan Bates Theatre); *The Misanthrope* (White Bear Theatre); *Hours Till Autumn* (Riverside Studios); *Art* (ADC Theatre, Cambridge); *Pause to Wonder* (Hen & Chickens); *Who's Afraid of Virginia Wade* (Old Vic 24 Hour Plays); *The Bacchae* (C-Venues Edinburgh); *Dracula* (C-Venues Edinburgh); *The New Magic Show* (C-Venues Edinburgh); *Singin' in the Rain* (Cambridge Arts Theatre).

This is Simon's first project as assistant director.

Simon is the Artistic Director of Black and White Rainbow.

James Farncombe (Lighting Designer)

Theatre for the Bush includes: *2000 Feet Away, The Whisky Taster, Tinderbox, The Dysfunctionalz, Crooked* and *I Like Mine with a Kiss.*

Other recent credits include *Juliet and her Romeo* (Bristol Old Vic); *Ghost Stories* (Lyric Hammersmith/West End); *The Overcoat* (Gecko Theatre/Lyric Hammersmith); *Dancing at Lughnasa* (Birmingham Rep); *The Winter's Tale* (UK tour for Schtanhaus in association with Headlong); *Adolf Hitler: My Part in His Downfall* (Rho Delta productions, Bristol Old Vic and tour); *The Great Game – Afghanistan* (a cycle of 12 new plays at the Tricycle, London); *Breaking the Silence* (Nottingham Playhouse).

James is a freelance designer, working throughout the UK.

James is an Associate Artist at the Bush. A full list of credits and production photographs are available at web.mac.com/jamesfarncombe.

Emma Laxton (Sound Designer)

Theatre for the Bush includes: *The Whisky Taster, If There Is I Haven't Found It Yet, 2nd May 1997, Apologia, The Contingency Plan, Wrecks, Broken Space Season, 2000 Feet Away, Tinderbox.*

Theatre for The Royal Court includes: *Off The Endz!, Tusk Tusk, Faces in the Crowd, That Face, Gone Too Far!, Catch, Scenes From The Back of Beyond, Woman and Scarecrow, The World's Biggest Diamond, Incomplete And Random Acts of Kindness, My Name Is Rachel Corrie* (also Minetta Lane, New York/Galway Festival/Edinburgh Festival), *Bone, The Weather, Bear Hug, Terrorism, Food Chain.*

West End theatre includes: *Treasure Island* (Theatre Royal Haymarket); *That Face* (Duke Of York's); *My Name Is Rachel Corrie* (Playhouse Theatre).

Other theatre includes: *Travels With My Aunt* (Northampton Royal); *Sisters* (Crucible Studio); *Ghosts* (ATC at Arcola Theatre); *Pornography* (Tricycle Theatre/ Birmingham Rep/Traverse, Edinburgh); *A Christmas Carol* (Chichester Festival Theatre);*Welcome to Ramallah* (iceandfire); *Shoot/Get Treasure/Repeat* (National Theatre); *Europe* (Dundee Rep/Barbican Pit); *Other Hands* (Soho Theatre); *The Unthinkable* (Sheffield Theatres); *My Dad is a Birdman* (Young Vic); *The Gods Are Not To Blame* (Tiata Fahodzi at Arcola Theatre).

Emma is an Associate Artist at the Bush.

Lucy Osborne (Designer)

Theatre for the Bush includes: *The Whisky Taster, If There Is I Haven't Found It Yet, Wrecks, Broken Space Festival, Sea Wall, 2,000 Feet Away, Tinderbox* and *tHe dYsFUnCKshOnalZ!*

Recent theatre credits include *The Taming of the Shrew* and *Twelfth Night* (for which she won Chicago 'Jeff Award' for Scenic Design) for the Chicago Shakespeare Theatre; *Playhouse Live: Here* (Sky Arts); *Andersen's English, Dreams of Violence* (Out of Joint); *Shades* (Royal Court's Young Writers Festival); *Macbeth* (Edinburgh Lyceum/Nottingham Playhouse); *Nina* and *Gas Station Angel* (repertoire, LAMDA); *Timing* (Kings Head) and *When Romeo Met Juliet* (BBC).

She designed *Artefacts* (nabokov Theatre Company / Bush) and *Some Kind of Bliss* (Trafalgar Studios), both of which transferred to the 2008 *'Brits off Broadway Festival'* in New York and other theatre credits include *Be My Baby* (New Vic Theatre); *Rope* (Watermill Theatre); *Closer* (Theatre Royal Northampton); *The Long and the Short and The Tall* (Sheffield Lyceum); *The Prayer Room* (Birmingham Rep/ Edinburgh Festival); *Ship of Fools* (set, Theatre 503); *The Unthinkable* (Sheffield Crucible Studio); and *Season of Migration to the North* (RSC New Writing Season).

Lucy graduated from Motley Theatre Design School in 2003, having also gained a BA in Fine Art from the University of Newcastle.

Lucy is an Associate Artist at the Bush.

Josie Rourke (Director)

Josie is Artistic Director of the Bush Theatre. She trained as Resident Assistant Director at the Donmar Warehouse, and was trainee Associate Director at the Royal Court and Associate Director of Sheffield Theatres.

Directing work for the Bush includes: *Apologia, Wrecks, 2,000 Feet Away, Tinderbox, How To Curse*, and *If There is I Haven't Found it Yet*.

Other theatre includes: *The Taming of the Shrew, Twelfth Night* (Chicago Shakespeare Theatre, nominated for six Jeff Awards); *Loyal Women, Crazyblackmuthafuckin'self* (Royal Court); *The Cryptogram, World Music, Frame 312* (Donmar Warehouse); *Believe What You Will, King John* (RSC); *My Dad's a Birdman* (Young Vic); *Romeo and Juliet* (Liverpool Playhouse).

Theatre for Sheffield Theatres: *The Long and the Short and the Tall, Much Ado About Nothing, The Unthinkable, World Music, Kick For Touch.*

She has also directed 24 hour Plays at The Old Vic and on Broadway.

Upcoming projects include: *Men Should Weep* (National Theatre).

Anthony Weigh (Writer)

Anthony graduated from the National Institute of Dramatic Art, Sydney in 1989 and since then has worked extensively as an actor both in Australia and internationally. In 2004 he undertook the Masters in Playwrighting at The University of Birmingham and was subsequently appointed Literary Manager at Australia's Company B, Belvoir St. Theatre in Sydney.

His first full length play, *2,000 Feet Away*, had its world premiere at Belvoir Street Theatre, Sydney and its UK premiere at the Bush, London directed by Josie Rourke. The play will have its American premiere in a production at Steep Theatre in Chicago in May 2010.

Other works include; *The Flooded Grave* (Bush); *Broad Street, or, How do I strike you?* (University of Birmingham 20/20 season).

In 2009 Anthony was appointed Playwright in Residence at the National Theatre in London and is currently an Associate Playwright at the Bush.

Like a Fishbone: An argument and an architectural model will open in a subsequent production at the Sydney Theatre Company in July 2010.

Awards and fellowships include; Australia Council for the Arts Emerging Artists Grant, Mick Young Playwrighting Award, Mike Walsh Fellowship, Helpmann Award and the Barry Jackson Scholarship at the University of Birmingham.

Anthony is currently under commission to: The National Theatre, Sydney Theatre Company, Melbourne Theatre Company, Malthouse Theatre.

The Bush Theatre

'One of the most experienced prospectors of raw talent in Europe'
The Independent

Since its inception in 1972, the Bush Theatre has pursued its singular vision of discovery, risk and entertainment from its home on the corner of Shepherds Bush Green. That vision is valued and embraced by a community of audience and artists radiating out from our distinctive corner of West London across the world. The Bush is a local theatre with an international reputation. From its beginning, the Bush has produced hundreds of groundbreaking premieres, many of them Bush commissions, and hosted guest productions by leading companies and artists from across the world. On any given night, those queuing at the foot of our stairs to take their seats could have travelled from Auckland or popped in from round the corner.

What draws them to the Bush is the promise of a good night out and our proven commitment to launch, from our stage, successive generations of playwrights and artists. Samuel Adamson, David Eldridge, Jonathan Harvey, Catherine Johnson, Tony Kushner, Stephen Poliakoff, Jack Thorne and Victoria Wood (all then unknown) began their careers at the Bush. The unwritten contract between talent and risk is understood by actors who work at the Bush, creating roles in untested new plays. Unique amongst local theatres, the Bush consistently draws actors of the highest reputation and calibre. Joseph Fiennes and Ian Hart recently took leading roles in a first play by an unknown playwright to great critical success. John Simm and Richard Wilson acted in premieres both of which transferred into the West End. The Bush has won over 100 awards, and developed an enviable reputation for touring its acclaimed productions nationally and internationally. Audiences and organisations far beyond our stage profit from the risks we take. The value attached to the Bush by other theatres and by the film and television industries is both significant and considerable. The Bush receives more than 1,000 scripts through the post every year, and reads and responds to them all. This is one small part of a comprehensive playwrights' development programme which nurtures the relationship between writer and director, as well as playwright residencies and commissions. Everything that we do to develop playwrights focuses them towards a production on our stage or beyond.

We have also launched an ambitious new education, training and professional development programme, bushfutures, providing opportunities for different sectors of the community and professionals to access the expertise of Bush playwrights, directors, designers, technicians and actors, and to play an active role in influencing the future development of the theatre and its programme. Last year saw the launch of our new social networking and online publishing website **www.bushgreen.org**. The site is a great new forum for playwrights and theatre people to meet, share experiences and collaborate. Through this pioneering work, the Bush will reach and connect with new writers and new audiences, and find new plays to stage.

Josie Rourke, Artistic Director

At the Bush

We're a full-time staff of eleven, supported by a big team of associates, interns, and freelancers. For ways to get involved, please look at our website www.bushtheatre.co.uk

***Artistic Director**	Josie Rourke
Executive Director	Angela Bond
Development Director	Trish Wadley
Box Office and Front of House Manager	Annette Butler
Marketing Manager	Sophie Coke-Steel
Producer	Caroline Dyott
Assistant to the Directors	Liz Eddy
Technical Manager	Neil Hobbs
Development Officer	Bethany Ann McDonald
Production Manager	Anthony Newton
Associate Director – bushfutures	Anthea Williams
Assistant Technician	Samuel Charleston
Bookkeeper	Ella Rule
Development Officer	Leonora Twynam
Associateships, Internships and Attachments	
Associate Director	Nathan Curry
Associate Director	Charlotte Gwinner
Pearson Writer in Residence	Nick Payne
Composer on attachment	Michael Bruce
Apprentice	Sade Banks
bushfutures Intern	Lucy McCann
Associate Playwright	Anthony Weigh
Creative Associates	Alice Lacey, Joe Murphy, Nessah Muthy, Richard Twynam, Ed Viney.
Associate Artists	Tanya Burns, Arthur Darvill, Chloe Emmerson, James Farncombe, Richard Jordan, Emma Laxton, Paul Miller, Lucy Osborne
Box Office Assistants	Kirsty Cox, Alex Hern, Kate McGregor, Ava Jade Morgan, Amanda Ramasawmy, Lee Simpson
Front of House Duty Managers	Sade Banks, Kirsty Cox, Alex Hern, Laurelle Jones, Lucy McCann, Kate McGregor, Ava Jade Morgan, Kirsty Patrick Ward, Jen Vile
Duty Technicians	Ben Ainsley, Vivienne Clavering, Adam McElderry, Ruth Perrin, Ben Sherratt
Press Representative	Ewan Thomson
Press Assistant	Ava Jade Morgan

* **Bold** text indicates full time staff, regular indicates part time/temporary.

The Bush Theatre, Shepherds Bush Green, London W12 8QD
Box Office: 020 8743 5050 | www.bushtheatre.co.uk

The Alternative Theatre Company Ltd. (The Bush Theatre) is a Registered Charity no. 270080

Company registration no. 1221968 | VAT no. 228 3168 73

Supported by ARTS COUNCIL ENGLAND

supported by h&f hammersmith & fulham

Be There at the Beginning

The Bush Theatre would like to say a very special 'Thank You' to the following supporters, corporate sponsors and trusts and foundations, whose valuable contributions continue to help us nurture, develop and present some of the brightest new literary stars and theatre artists.

If you are interested in finding out how to be involved, visit the 'Support Us' section of our website, email development@bushtheatre.co.uk or call 020 8743 3584.

Lone Star
Eric Abraham & Sigrid Rausing
Gianni Alen-Buckley
Michael Alen-Buckley
Catherine Johnson
Caryn Mandabach
Christopher Hampton

Handful of Stars
Anonymous
Jim Broadbent
Clyde Cooper
David & Alexander Emmerson
Tom Erhardt
Chris & Sofia Fenichell
Julia Foster
Douglas Kennedy
Tarel & Diala Khlat
Richard and Elizabeth Phillips
Alan Rickman
John & Tita Shakeshaft

Glee Club
Anonymous
John Botrill
David Brooks
Maggie Burrows
Clive Butler
Matthew Byam Shaw
Vivien Goodwin
Simon Johnson
Paul & Cathy Kafka
Neil LaBute
Brian Smith

Corporate Sponsors
The Agency (London) Ltd
Curtis Brown Group Ltd
Fredereck Sage Co. Ltd.
Harbottle & Lewis LLP
Ludgate Environmental Ltd
Markson Pianos
West12 Shopping & Leisure Centre
Westfield London

Trusts and Foundations
The Daisy Trust
The D'Oyly Carte Charitable Trust
The Earls Court & Olympia Charitable Trust
The Elizabeth & Gordon Bloor Charitable Foundation
The Eranda Foundation
Garfield Weston Foundation
The Gatsby Charitable Foundation
Haberdashers' Benevolent Foundation
The Harold Hyam Wingate Foundation
Jerwood Charitable Foundation
The John Thaw Foundation
The Laurie & Gillian Marsh Charitable Trust
The Leverhulme Trust
The Marina Kleinwort Trust
The Martin Bowley Charitable Trust
Old Possum's Practical Trust
The Peggy Ramsay Foundation
The Peter Wolff Theatre Trust
The Thistle Trust
Split Infinitive Trust
The 2011 Trust

The Bush Theatre has the support of the Pearson Playwrights' Scheme, sponsored by the Peggy Ramsay Foundation

---

bushfutures

bushfutures is a programme that allows our community and emerging practitioners and playwrights to access the work of the Bush.

bushcontenders

Over 60 and love the theatre? Nearly went for it but life got in the way?

bushcontenders is a new year round acting programme for everyone who could have been a contender. Members will receive discounted tickets to selected Saturday matinees and take part in an acting workshop with case and directors here at the Bush following the performance. There is not charge for the workshop, all you need is to register in advance.

bushcontenders for *Like a Fishbone* - 19 June.

bushactivists

bushactivists is a group for young people aged 15–20 who live, work or study in Hammersmith and Fulham. Activists will have the chance to see what happens behind the scenes here at the theatre and receive a free ticket for one selected performance of each show here at the Bush. On the day of the performance, activists will take part in a fun pre-performance workshop before seeing the show as a group.

bushactivists for *Like a Fishbone* – 16 June.

Missed it? Come to bushactivists for *Great British Country Fete* – 4 August

A Night Less Ordinary

Under 26? Like getting a freebie? Then you've come to the right place.

As part of a new Arts Council England scheme (in association with Metro), the Bush is offering free theatre tickets to those aged 25 and under (one free ticket available per person per year, subject to availability). So if you fancy A Night Less Ordinary, and want to see some of the best new shows in London call us on 020 8743 5050 for more details and to book tickets.

To find out more about bushfutures contact
bushfutures@bushtheatre.co.uk
or call Anthea Williams on 020 8743 3584

Anthony Weigh

Like a Fishbone

An argument and
an architectural model

ff

faber and faber

First published in 2010
by Faber and Faber Limited
74–77 Great Russell Street
London WC1B 3DA

Typeset by Country Setting, Kingsdown, Kent CT14 8ES
Printed in England by CPI Bookmarque, Croydon, Surrey

A CIP record for this book
is available from the British Library

978–0–571–26975–4

2 4 6 8 10 9 7 5 3 1

Characters

The Architect
an older woman

The Mother
a younger woman

The Intern
a young woman

A Child
a girl

LIKE A FISHBONE

To call on them to give up their illusion about their condition is to call on them to give up a condition that requires illusions.

Karl Marx

Their monument sticks like a fishbone
in the city's throat.

Robert Lowell, 'For the Union Dead'

An oblique stroke (/) indicates that the following character should begin speaking simultaneously at this point.

Children singing in the distance. Their voices come and go on the shifting breeze.

Winter rain against a large window.

On a table an architectural scale model of a small town. At its centre a little rise and a model schoolhouse; one entire wall of the model schoolhouse is see-through. A clear Perspex box covers the entire model town.

A woman, the Mother; long skirt, long blouse, long wet hair tied back with a scarf, looks 'out of time'.

The Architect, dressed for the/an occasion, blinking as if a light has been switched on suddenly in a darkened room.

Long pause.

Mother Are you a lady?

Pause.

Hello?

Architect I . . . I'm –

Mother They told me to stay here.

Architect They?

Mother Downstairs. I –

Architect Downstairs?

Mother A man / told me to . . .

Architect A man . . .?

Mother Yes. At the front.

Architect There's a man / at the front?

Mother He told me . . . put me in here.

Architect He put you . . . ?

Mother He told me to wait in here.

Architect To wait?

Mother Yes. He said / to wait.

Architect To wait.

Mother Smells in here.

Architect Sorry?

Mother Smells of glue.

Architect Sorry. Smells?

Mother In here. Smells of glue.

Pause.

Architect (*suddenly realising*) Yes. That's for the . . . the models . . . for gluing things . . . one to another . . . for . . . I'm sorry, how is it I can / help?

Mother I'm wet.

Architect Yes.

Mother It's raining.

Architect Yes.

Mother I came up by train. Only it wasn't a train. It was a bus. Rail replacement. Track works. Because of the flooding. It rained all the way.

Architect Did it.

Mother When I got here a lady at the station gave me her elbow to here. She had an umbrella but it didn't do any good.

Architect Yes.

Mother You're near the station, aren't you?

Architect Are we?

Mother It didn't seem far.

Architect I suppose we're near the station.

Mother Then the man downstairs put me in here. To wait. He said 'sit down' but I didn't want to. I'm wet.

Architect Yes.

Mother I didn't want to make things wet.

Pause.

Architect (*suddenly realising*) I'm sorry . . . Yes, of course . . . Let's . . . we should have a . . . I've got a towel . . . some towel . . . there *should* be some anyway. (*Searching.*) It's just that it's late and I thought I was the only one here.

Mother I'm here.

Architect I was expecting someone else.

Mother The man told me to –

Architect You startled me, that's all.

Mother I'm sorry.

Architect Here . . . it's not much . . . it's a . . . it's some towel. Here.

She holds out a roll of paper towel from somewhere.
The Mother remains still.
The Architect realises her mistake – the Mother is only partially sighted. She touches the Mother with the towel, causing her to jump a bit.

Sorry. Here. Sorry.

The Mother takes the towel and dries her face.
The Architect looks at her watch.
The Mother holds out the used towel for the Architect.

Mother Thank you.

Architect I'll take that then, shall I?

Mother You smell nice.

Architect I . . . ?

Mother Rain's heavy.

Architect Yes.

Mother You get used to the wet living down there . . .

Architect / Down?

Mother . . . Still. Good for the cheese.

Architect Sorry. Cheese?

Mother Rain. Good for the grass. Good for the cows. Good for the cheese.

Architect Yes, of course. The cheese. It's what you're known for down there, isn't it. Of course.

Mother Yes.

Architect Yes.

Mother And the school.

Architect Pardon me?

Mother Now. We're known for the school. Aren't we?

Architect Yes.

Pause.

Mother Are we waiting then?

Architect Sorry. Are we . . .?

Mother For the architect.

Architect I'm sorry?

Mother I'm here for the architect.

Architect You are?

Mother That's what I told the man downstairs. It's why he put me in here. He said it was late but that he should still be here.

Architect He?

Mother The architect.

Architect You're waiting for / the architect?

Mother The architect, yes.

Architect I'm an architect.

Mother I thought . . . I want to speak to the architect.

Architect Yes. And I'm –

Mother No. I'm sorry, but . . . *The* architect. I'm sorry.

Architect The . . .?

Mother *The* architect. The man said he should still be here.

Architect I don't . . .

Pause.
Suddenly the Mother tries to make her way to the door.

Mother This must be a mistake. / I should. He said that he should still be here. That it's late but that he should still be here.

Architect It's alright. Really . . . There seems to have been some . . . I'm the architect . . . you see?

Pause.

Mother What?

Architect I'm *the* architect.

Pause.

Mother I thought. I thought. I'm sorry, but you're a lady.

Architect Yes. You can be both.

Mother Both?

Architect A lady and an architect. A lady architect. A . . . never mind.

Mother I thought . . . he said 'he'.

Architect Well, I'm a she.

Mother I'm embarrassed.

Architect It's alright.

Mother I'm . . . I'm . . . I'm –

Suddenly the Mother lurches forward as if to faint.

Architect Wait! Here . . . you're . . . here . . . there's a chair here . . .

Mother I'm wet.

Architect No you're not. You're dry now. It's alright.

Mother I thought . . . I thought . . .

Architect It's alright. It doesn't matter. Put your head between your knees.

Mother I haven't stopped since I left.

Architect You've come a long way. Put your head . . . That's it.

Mother I've come a long way.

Architect Yes.

Mother And I thought you were –

Architect It doesn't matter. Really. Take a deep breath. Good. And out. And another. And out. Good.

Mother Yes.

Architect You're shivering. Are you cold . . . ?

Mother / No.

Architect Do you want a cup of something? Warm you up? / Would you?

Mother I could have a cup of water

Architect I'm pretty sure I can arrange that. A cup of water? There's biscuits here too somewhere. Do you want a biscuit?

Mother Alright.

The Architect finds a bottle of water and a packet of biscuits. Perhaps she finds a plate and arranges the biscuits.

Architect I keep them here for emergencies.

Mother Emergencies?

Architect Just in case I get an attack of the munchies. Late at night. If we're working. They're a bit grim but . . . here you go. They're . . . they're just here. I'll put them on the table for you. And a cup of water. Here.

Mother Thank you.

She eats.

The Architect checks her watch.

Architect That's a pretty scarf.

Mother It's . . . thank you.

She drinks.

Architect Gosh. You *are* thirsty.

Mother I haven't eaten all day.

Architect That was silly of you.

Mother I didn't think to. I just came.

Architect I forget to eat sometimes too.

Mother It felt too important to eat.

Architect Goodness.

Mother The bus stopped. Twice. But I didn't want to get off in case I couldn't get back on.

Architect Well. You should eat.

Mother Yes.

Architect Feel better?

Mother Yes.

Architect Got your breath back?

Mother Yes. Thank you. You're very kind.

Architect You take as long as you need. (*She checks her watch.*)

Mother Thank you.

Architect Alright?

Mother Yes.

Architect You sure?

Mother Yes.

Pause.

Architect Listen to that rain.

Mother Yes.

Pause.

Architect So.

Mother Sorry?

Architect So. How is it I can / help you?

Mother My daughter sent me.

Architect Your . . .? / Your daughter . . .

Mother Yes.

Architect . . . And do we know your daughter?

Mother I don't think so.

Architect She's not on the . . . she can't be on the project board.

Mother No.

Architect And so she sent you.

Mother Yes. To speak to the architect.

Architect To me.

Mother No. Yes. To the architect. To you. Yes.

Architect You could have just rung me up. It's a long way.

Mother Yes. Yes, I could have. But . . . no, she said I needed to see you.

Architect Alright. You're seeing me . . . here . . . with me. What can I / do for you?

Mother I want to see it.

Architect Pardon me?

Mother I want to see it.

Architect It?

Mother You know, the . . . the . . .

Architect I don't . . .

Mother The monument.

Pause.

Hello . . .?

Architect Yes.

Mother I want to see it.

Architect Pardon me, but. You want to see . . .?

Mother For you to tell it to me. To show me. To explain it.

Architect I see.

Mother My daughter said that if I'm so worried I should come here and ask to speak to you –

Architect / And here you are.

Mother – and . . . and to ask you to show it to me. To tell me about it.

Architect I see. Worried, you said?

Mother No. Interested.

Architect Interested.

Mother Yes.

Pause.

Architect Do you know anyone on the project board?

Mother Some of the . . . / some of the people from our . . .

Architect And you didn't think to speak to them?

Mother . . . No! No, my daughter said to speak to you. That I had to speak to you.

Architect Had to?

Mother Should. Should speak to you.

Architect I mean that's what a project board is for. Isn't it? In these situations. To take information back to the stakeholders.

Mother Stake—?

Architect Interested . . . parties.

Mother I'm an interested party.

Architect I know that. I knew that when I first saw you. I knew who you were.

Mother I haven't met you before.

Architect No. I knew where you were from, though.

Mother Yes.

Architect And you've come all that way up here in a train to talk to me?

Mother No.

Architect No?

Mother It was a bus.

Architect A bus, sorry.

Mother My daughter told me –

Architect There are two . . . no . . . three people on the project board from your . . . your / community?

Mother Church. I know that.

Architect . . . Yes? Have they not been feeding stuff back? Have your people . . . your church . . . people not been feeding stuff back?

Mother No. I mean . . . yes . . . yes, they do. They come back from the meetings you have. But I . . . I don't . . . any of it. And my daughter said you would help. Help me to understand.

Architect I see.

Pause.

Look . . . would you wait just one minute?

Mother Alright.

Architect Don't go anywhere.

Mother Go . . .?

Architect Just . . . sit tight.

The Architect leaves the room.
The Mother.
The Architect returns with another chair.
She also has a mobile phone which she places on the table between them.
She sits opposite the Mother.

Architect How are you feeling?

Mother Good.

Architect Good. Good.
So. Let me say from the outset that we don't have a lot of time. Tonight is important.

Mother Alright.

Architect So. You understand that in a situation / such as yours . . .

Mother A situation?

Architect . . . Tragedy. Yes. Such as took place in your town. In a situation such as that there are a lot of people who feel they have a stake –

Mother The stakeholders.

Architect That's right. And they all have needs. Yes?

Mother Yes.

Architect We recognise that . . . recognised it.

Mother I don't know what you're saying.

Architect Yes. And I'm telling you.
What normally happens when someone . . . a firm . . . a practice such as ours say . . . is commissioned to design an important / memorial –

Mother Monument.

Architect – such as yours, is that we would receive the brief.

Mother Brief?

Architect Brief, yes. From the stakeholders. Yes?

Mother Alright.

Architect Then we would arrive in your town and take interviews, as we did, and measurements and photographs, lots of photographs, and survey the site –

Mother The school.

Architect The school, yes, as we did . . . and then go away . . . come back here to the city and engage engineers and landscape architects and the like, and then six months later . . . more or less . . . well . . . present something to you.

Mother Something?

Architect Exactly! Some edifice or some statue or something.

Mother Yes! A statue.

Architect Well. In the light of. Because there are so very many stakeholders . . . we wanted to work a different way. So, we proposed / a process.

Mother Process.

Architect Process. / That's right.

Mother *That's* the word they said when they came back from the meetings. / That it was going to be a process.

Architect That's right. Instead of a . . . an edifice. That way *you'd* control the outcome. *You'd* own it. We . . . we . . . we've spent the last six months . . . facilitating . . . leading you –

Mother Not me.

Architect No. The project board . . . remember? Made up of the stakeholders . . . people from your community . . . church . . . and the government – culture, media, heritage, tourism –

Mother Tourism?

Architect Yes. Because of its significance, not just to you but to the nation . . . and that's the point I'm trying to make rather . . . rather, well . . . badly . . . that we created a project board to facilitate the process of the design and *also* to pass on . . . back . . . to you what was happening. That's what I'm saying. You see? You and your daughter . . . you should be speaking to the project board.

Mother I'm speaking to you.

Pause.

Architect Are you sure you wouldn't rather . . . ?

Pause.

No.

The Architect checks her watch.
She picks up the phone and looks at it.

Right! So. We . . . we led . . . led you . . . them . . . the project board . . . through a process which has produced this. (*'That should do shouldn't it?'*)

Pause.

Mother What?

Architect A conservation of the site.

Mother The school.

Architect The school, yes.

Mother Conservation.

Architect Yes.

Mother I don't understand.

Architect A conserv— Like . . . like – (*and seizing on something*) jam. You know?

Mother I don't understand.

Architect Well . . . It *is* like jam really. Where jam was once plums or raspberries or oranges and is . . . well . . . is still those things but is now those things but in a different form.

Mother Oranges?

Architect We will take the site –

Mother School.

Architect School, yes? We will take it and very carefully, very respectfully preserve it. Conserve it.

Mother Like jam.

Architect Yes like jam. Exactly as it was that day. Every upturned desk, every dropped pencil case, every crushed crayon, every scattered piece of chalk, every broken chair, every scuff mark. So that people. People today and . . . and in the future can come to your town and . . . and . . . go to the site . . . the school . . . and . . . and say to themselves: 'What happened here? Where are the children? Where have all the children gone?' The building becomes a kind of question mark. You see? Like jam was plums but is now plum jam, your site was once a school but is now a memorial. The same but different. You're shivering.

Mother Yes . . . I'm . . . I'm . . . People come down now, you know.

Architect People . . .?

Mother On the weekends.

Architect Yes. We know.

And getting her coat and placing it around the Mother's shoulders.

Here, have my –

Mother Thank you. Hundreds of them. You know? They park their cars anywhere. All over the place. Like a . . . like a . . . like a . . . ants. Just to get a look at where it happened. Just to . . . just to . . .

Architect Yes.

Mother They can't get close now because of those . . . the fences you put up around it, but it doesn't stop them coming. Wave after wave after wave. / Locals know not to come into town on a weekend. Know they'll never find a place to park.

Architect Waves of them. Yes, I understand. We know. It's how people are . . . they're naturally curious, aren't they? They want to see.

Mother Better once it's pulled down.

Architect Sorry?

Mother Be better for us once it's gone.

Architect Um. No. I'm sorry, but you don't . . . The thing is, to preserve . . . to conserve means that we keep the building. Actually.

Mother You keep it?

Architect We . . . very, carefully. Very, respectfully –

Mother How can you do that then?

Architect How . . .?

Mother I don't understand that. How is that possible? The building? How is that possible? To preserve. To conserve. Like jam. I don't see that . . . how you could do that? I don't see how you could do that.

Pause.

Are you . . .?

The Architect checks her watch.

Architect That rain's easing, isn't it?

Pause.

It's a very complicated –

The Architect's phone rings.
She jumps to answer it.

Hello? . . . Hello, can you? . . . For some reason . . . It's the rain . . . I can't . . . Can you hear me? . . . . . . Can you? . . . Hello? . . . I'm in the . . . Hello?

Dead.

Sorry.

Pause.

Look!

She suddenly pushes her chair back and begins to take the Perspex cover off the model. The Mother is alarmed and stands up, sending her chair falling backwards and the coat from her shoulders.

Mother What are you . . .?

Architect If I could just show you . . . to . . . to . . . to help you, yes? / To help you to understand what it is I'm talking about . . .

Mother What are you doing? What is that? What is that?

The Architect has prised the model school house from the little town and is trying to place it in the Mother's hand.

Architect . . . If you'd . . . if you'd hold out your hand / . . . No . . . no, it's alright . . . no . . . no, please . . . please, no . . . it's . . . I'm not trying to . . . please . . . please . . . it's just . . . please . . . please hold out . . . No . . . no . . . you don't understand . . . It's just . . . it's nothing . . . it's just . . .

Mother Please . . . don't . . . what are you doing? What are you doing? Don't, please . . . no . . . no, I don't want you to. Don't . . . that's . . . that's . . . what is that?! What is this?! What . . .?! What . . .?!

The Mother has the model.

Architect There.

Mother What's . . .? This is . . . this is like . . . is this?

Architect Yes.

Mother This is a toy.

Architect Model, yes.

Mother A . . . a . . . a doll's house.

Architect Or a school house? Perhaps? A little church school house?

Mother A little church . . .? This is the . . .?

Architect School.

Mother School?

Architect Made in a factory and transported down there in the – what? Seventy-six? Seven? Prefab structure set on a concrete plinth. North–south axis to make the most of the sun coming up the valley. Four windows. One door. Firetrap really . . .

Mother / A trap?

Architect . . . More like a glorified shed really, isn't it? Only ever meant to be / temporary . . .

Mother Preserved.

Architect . . . Exactly! Like jam. With the whole south wall taken off and reimagined in glass so that people can see in. Now, if you'll let me –

The Architect moves toward the Mother.
The Mother senses this and moves away.

Mother Do you believe in God?

Architect I'm sorry?

Mother Do you believe in God?

Architect Do I . . .?

Mother Believe in God. Yes.

Architect Um. No.

Mother What do you believe in then?

Architect Gosh. Myself. The truth. Humanity.

Mother Human killed my daughter.

Architect I know, but . . .

Mother / No 'but' to that.

Architect I'm sorry. You? Did you say your daughter?

Mother Died with the rest.

Architect I thought you said . . .?

Mother One of the first to go, they said. How they can tell that from holes in her head I don't know.

Architect Your daughter is dead?

Mother With the rest. Yes. She has visited me. Talked to me. And . . .

She holds the model school out at arm's length for the Architect.

We don't want this.

Black.

The rain has eased.

The Architect is trying to open the window.

The Intern has replaced the Mother.

She holds the model school.

Architect . . . And I don't even know why I'm telling you this . . . but, when I was a girl I didn't have posters of pop stars on my walls like the other girls. Yes? I had a picture of Richard Seifert's design for Centrepoint. Centrepoint, for God's sake! I was meant to be doing my homework, but I'd steal into my father's drafting studio and swipe his pens and paper and things and . . . I'd get a hiding for it afterwards . . . but in the meantime I'd be drawing airports and train stations and shipping terminals, museums, concert halls, art galleries, seats of government, sporting arenas. Mapping the flow of people . . . ingress and egress. The great buildings of our time. Yes? Are these . . . ? What? Are these painted shut?

Getting a tool to help.

All embodiments of the great progressive ideas of our time. Environmentalism, liberalism, rejectivism, pacifism, secularism, humanism. Yes? In the West, at least. That's what a great building is, isn't it? A progressive idea you're walking around inside of. I mean. No one goes, 'I'm going to start a war, but first let's build a glorious building for it,' or, 'Gosh, I want to torture the populace, but first let's build an especially beautiful building to do that in, shall we?' or, 'I wouldn't mind eavesdropping on our citizens, could you design me an elegant tower for that?' Or . . . yes . . . OK . . . there were the gas chambers . . . but they were barely buildings at all . . . Slabs of . . . of . . . of ugly. For God's sake!

The window. Another approach.

No. It's generally, 'I want to hear some music . . . I want to look at a painting . . . I want to learn about my country . . . I want to read a book . . . I want to run a race . . . Can you build me a building for that, please?' And, here's my point, in a hundred years' time *these* are the relics we will point to to show who we are . . . were. Not. Not, well frankly, the churches and office towers and things my father was known for. No, it's . . . *These* are the buildings that we'll point to . . . to prove our civility, our humanity. Our . . . on the whole . . . humanness. God! (*The window.*) Our non-apeness.

Intern Non-ape?

Architect We are not animals.

Intern No.

Architect The alpha and omega.

Intern Yes.

Architect That we build such buildings proves it.

Intern I'm an animal.

Architect What?

She is stopped in her tracks by the argument and the window.

Intern I'm an animal. My boyfriend says I *eat* like an animal.

Pause.

I'm sorry. Was that . . .? I'm sorry. I was trying to be . . . Sorry. I interrupted. Sorry. Go on.

Pause.

Architect I suppose I should say thank you.

Intern If you like.

Architect Thank you.

Intern I was here for the model.

Architect I know, but, the timing.

Intern It's my job, isn't it?

Architect They tell me I'm on some sort of register.

Intern Register?

Architect A register of risk. A risk register. For tonight.

Intern What? For the presentation?

Architect Because of the nature of the . . . The religious nature / of the thing . . . the act . . . unbelievable . . .

Intern What? Because he was a . . .? That sad man? / Who went into the school?

Architect I suppose so, yes.

Intern That's –

Architect I know. So, when I saw her I thought, 'Hello.'

Intern Of course.

Architect I'm sure the blood drained right out of my face. I must have looked like a sheet. To walk in and just find her here. Standing.

Intern Of course.

Architect She said a man put her in here.

Intern A man?

Architect Downstairs.

Intern There's a man downstairs?

Architect That's what I said.

Intern When I heard voices I assumed . . .

Architect Thank goodness.

Intern I was coming to get the model. So.

Architect Just as well.

Intern Do you want anything else?

Architect Do I . . .?

Intern It's . . . We don't have much time.

Architect Yes. Yes, I'm sorry. Of course. Please don't let me. Of course. You better get that back on.

Of the model. She proceeds to.

Intern Yes.

Architect Don't worry about me. It's just that / I thought I was the only one here, and –

Intern I'm glad I've got this . . . I'm sorry . . . I interrupted. You thought . . .?

Architect No. No, it's fine. I'm being silly. You're glad . . .?

Intern I've got this opportunity.

Architect To . . .?

Intern Say thank you.

Architect For . . .?

Intern The opportunity.

Architect Oh.

Intern Now that it's all over.

Architect Well. That's our pleasure.

Intern This is my lift moment, isn't it?

Architect Your . . .?

Intern In Hollywood. And you've suddenly gotten in the lift with the movie producer and you've got thirty seconds to pitch them the film.

Architect I'm not following.

Intern I wouldn't normally get to be in a lift with you.

Architect We don't have a lift.

Intern Metaphorically.

Architect I see.

Intern And now I am, I just wanted to take the opportunity to say thank you.

Architect Well. As I said. That's our –

Intern It's that thing from before, isn't it. That you always say.

Architect What do I always . . .?

Intern About Centrepoint. I'm the same as you. When I was a girl. Except for me. It was you. That's embarrassing, but. When I was a girl. Your design for the –

Architect Gosh!

Intern And having this opportunity has been – Well, it's been amazing. Watching and learning. Through the process. It's . . . well . . . *amazing*.

Architect Goodness. That's –

Intern How's that? (*The restored model.*)

Architect That's . . .? *Amazing*.

Intern Good.

Architect We should –

Mother (*off*) Hello?

Pause.
The two women look at each other. Who is going to speak first?

(*Off.*) Hello . . . is there . . .? Hello?

Long pause.

Intern (*calling out*) Here. We're in here. (*To Architect.*) Do you want me to . . .?

Architect Yes. You better.

Intern Just a . . .

She goes out.
The Architect alone.
The Intern returns with the Mother, who is wearing the Architect's coat.

Just watch the . . . There's a chair . . .

Mother Thank you.

Architect You survived, then.

Mother I'm sorry. I haven't been all day.

Intern You've come a long way.

Architect She certainly has, and in a bus.

Intern I hate buses. Always get sick on them. You know? It's those drivers, isn't it? With their feet on the pedal. On, off, on, off. All that braking. Makes me feel sick, doesn't it.

Pause.

Architect Yes.

Intern Well. I better get this over there.

Mother What . . .?

Intern The model. Of your . . . For tonight. For the presentation. I assumed –

Architect Yes, why don't you –

Intern You must be really pleased.

Mother Pleased?

Intern The memorial.

Mother It's just the school.

Intern Yes, but –

Architect Can we get you . . . Do you want something? Some . . . a tea or a coffee / or something . . .?

Mother I'll have a tea then.

Architect A tea . . . (*To Intern.*) Do you think you could . . . / would you mind?

Intern But we don't have much time. I have to get this –

Architect Just quickly.

Intern If you want me to.

Architect Do you take / milk and sugar?

Mother Just black.

Architect You're easy, aren't you?

Mother I just like my tea black.

Architect Good. Good, well if you could . . .

Intern Would you like . . .?

Architect No. / As you say, we need to get going.

Intern Black tea then.

Mother Yes.

Intern Right. I'll . . . I'll be back.

Architect I certainly hope so. / With that tea.

Intern Yes. (*To Mother.*) Good to see you. Meet you.

Pause.

I'll be . . .

And she's gone.
Long pause.

Mother She an architect?

Architect She . . .? She's a baby one. She's an intern. Do you know . . .? A sort of . . . training. She's very lucky to have a position like this. People would kill to do the sorts of things we have her doing.

Mother Getting tea?

Architect Yes. No. It's how it works. I had to do it. Even in – I worked for my father's practice and I had to do it.

Mother Your father was an / architect?

Architect Yes.

Mother . . . He must be proud of you then.

Architect I don't. We don't . . . possibly . . . I don't know.

Pause.

You do understand / that this is a very important –

Mother I'm not mad.

Architect I'm sorry?

Mother I am not mad.

Architect No. No, of course –

Mother I know that you think I am –

Architect No. It's just that –

Mother Crazy woman come here out of the wet. / Come here with stories about being sent. By her daughter.

Architect This is a very important evening for us and we really don't have much time.

Mother When a man loses a child I think he loses a . . . what's it called? The idea of something. The future of something. What could have been. It's a blow to him. That's why he cries. A blow to *him*.

Architect I –

Mother When a woman loses a child it's different to that. The child is resurrected every night in that woman's dreams, then killed fresh every morning a minute or two after waking when the woman comes to and realises the truth of her life now. The child. Born every night in dream. Killed every morning in waking. Over and over and over . . .

Architect / I can only imagine.

Mother All you do is sleep, you know.

Architect Yes.

Mother To try to get to your child. Sleep. To reach her. Then you wake up and the wall is there again between you and you realise. And the pit of your stomach goes.

Architect I can't begin to . . . are you hot / in here?

Mother Do you know the smell of children?

Architect The / smell?

Mother That was how I knew.

Architect I'm sorry. Knew . . .?

Mother At first I thought I was sleeping. I thought: 'This is the same as every other night. A dream of her.' But, it was the smell of her. Filling the room . . . like . . . like . . . I'd know that smell anywhere. The smell of your child. And the heaviness of her on the mattress. And I opened my eyes. And there she was. Is. My daughter. Crossed that wall between. Between us and sitting on the end of my bed. Sitting there and smelling like . . . like –

Architect I understand.

Mother And wet.

Architect Wet?

Mother Wet through.

Architect Why wet?

Mother Don't know. Head to foot. Dripping wet as if she'd just been pulled from a river.

Architect The River Styx perhaps.

Mother What?

Architect No. Nothing, it's a – Nothing.

Mother She talks to me. All night long. Sitting there and talking and talking. Never stopping. Never drawing a breath. Telling me things. Things about. The sort of things you would never credit. Just. Things. About that day. About what it was like that day. In the classroom. How all the children held hands. With each other. When he came in. How he made them stand in a line. How the big ones protected the little ones. With their bodies. How they were all –

Architect Victims, yes. Awful. I understand.

Mother No.

Architect No?

Mother No, you don't understand.

Architect Sorry, I'm trying to –

Mother Heroes.

Architect Heroes?

Mother My daughter. All of them. Heroes.

Architect But –

The Intern is in the room with the tea.

Intern Tea! I'll just . . . I'm sorry, am I . . . ?

Architect Not at all. We were just . . .

Intern I'll put it down here, shall I?

Architect Rain seems to have eased.

Intern A bit, yes.

Architect Good.

Intern I love the rain. Don't you love the rain?

Architect Um. Yes.

Intern Great for sleeping. Nothing better than hearing it on the window in the night. What about you? You like the rain?

Mother If I'm not in it.

Intern Of course –

Architect Thanks for the tea.

Intern And just so you know. The taxi's on its way.

Architect Taxi?

Intern I'll . . . I thought. It's raining. I know it's not far. To the hotel. But safer to get this over there. I thought. And there should be room for all of us –

Architect All . . . ?

Intern Yes. I assumed. To the hotel. In this rain. It might be easier for you both –

Architect Oh. No, no. It's only us. You and I. Our . . . our friend here is – I'm sorry. I should have made that clear.

Intern I assumed –

Architect Actually, why don't we . . . (*To the Mother.*) Let's call you a taxi. Shall we call you a taxi? It's still raining. Just. Let us call you a taxi to get you back to the station. We can't have you wet again. Yes? Yes. Would you mind? Calling a taxi? Another taxi –

Intern One for us and one for –

Architect Yes. So she doesn't get wet again. Heading back to the station. (*To Mother.*) We'll get you a taxi. Alright?

Intern I'll call another taxi then.

Architect Would you? One for us and one for –

Intern Alright.

Architect Thanks.

The Intern's gone.

How's your tea then?

Mother I haven't had any yet.

Architect Good. Good.

Mother Will you . . .?

Architect Yes?

Mother I want to ask you something.

Architect (*checking her watch*) Yes?

Mother Pray with me.

Architect I'm sorry, I don't –

Mother Don't need belief to pray.

Architect I'm sorry / but I think perhaps you do.

Mother All you need to do is to make the . . . the shape of it.

Architect Shape?

Mother The shadow. Shadow of a prayer. / That's all you need.

Architect But I don't. I'm not a believer. I don't mean to be disrespectful, but it would be . . . hollow . . . um, dishonest . . .

Mother You don't need to mean it.

Architect I wouldn't. Be meaning it.

Mother Why are you afraid?

Architect I'm not afraid.

Mother All I'm asking is that you pray with me.

Architect But that's quite a large thing to ask, isn't it.

Mother Is it?

Architect To me it is. To someone who doesn't. I'm sorry. I respect you. I really do. I appreciate the fact that you believe. That's fine. If that's what you . . . Really, that's fine by me. But I'd appreciate perhaps if you'd leave me to my beliefs . . . my *not* believing. If that's alright by you.

The Mother has stood and found her way to the Architect.

She takes her hand in what the Architect assumes to be a sort of handshake.

What are you . . .? Oh, I see. Good, good. Well, it's been great to meet you.

The Mother has both the Architect's hands now.

Mother Your hands are rough.

Architect Are they?

Mother Yes.

Architect That's the . . . too much time outside, I'm afraid. Building sites. My ex-husband used to say . . .

Mother Just . . .

The Mother presses the Architect's hands between her own.

That's all. Just the shape. Like this. That's all. You don't need to be frightened. That's it. To be a channel. Simple. Now. Father. Hear my prayer. Sanctify these hands. Use them –

Suddenly the Intern returns.

Intern Done!

Architect That was quick!

As the Architect pulls away she knocks the cup of tea over on the table. It wets a portion of the still-uncovered model town.

Hell! / The model! Quick! There's some towel! There! Yes! Quick! Just grab it! Yes.

Intern / No! Is there some . . . (*paper towel*)? Here? I've got it, I've got it, I've got it! It's just a little spill. Tiny. It's alright.

Architect It's fine.

Intern It's fine.

Architect Yes. It's fine.

Intern Lucky.

During the following the Mother, having been alerted to the existence of the model, feels her way to the table and begins to explore the uncovered model town.

Architect Bit of excitement. Sorry about your tea.

Intern I can make another if you –

Architect No! No, sadly we're really going to have to get –

Intern There's a bit of a wait with the rain now, I'm afraid.

Architect A wait?

Intern The taxis.

Architect There can't be.

Intern With the rain.

Architect But there can't be. We have to get away. To go. To get this over there. To –

Intern They said first available.

Architect Right. Well. Just as long as they know. Understand. That we have to go. That it *is* 'first available'.

Intern That's what they said.

Architect Alright. Well, I suppose there's nothing much we can –

Intern Shall I take that?

Architect What? Yes. Yes, thanks.

Handing her the lump of sodden paper towel.

Intern I'll call you when they're here.

Architect Yes. Please. As soon as. Please.

Intern Lucky. (*The sodden towel.*)

Architect Well done.

Intern Thanks.

Architect Bravo.

The Intern goes.

The thing is, we have this thing. This. With the memorial. Your memorial. Like she said. Tonight. Presenting it. Here. At a – It's a hotel. Nearby. It's not important where, is it, but it's a very significant night for us, incredibly significant, so, I'm sorry, but I'm going to have to ask you to –

The Mother is touching the model.

Please! Please be . . .!

Mother So, this is . . .

Architect Um. Your town.

Mother This is our town.

Architect This is your town, yes. I have to ask you to –

Mother This is what it looks like?

Architect Pretty much. Yes. Just. Bigger. Obviously.

Mother Not much, is it?

Architect Well, it's small, if that's what you mean. A small town.

Mother This is our main street? With the shops?

Architect Yes.

Mother And this?

Architect Yes. / That's your –

Mother This is the library, yes?

Architect / That's your library.

Mother Only open Mondays and Thursdays. Get in talking books for me. Specially. Why I was there. That day. / That Thursday. When we heard.

Architect Please be careful there!

Mother And this?

Architect That . . . that's the council . . . municipal building.

Mother So, this must be –

Architect That . . . that's the road.

Mother The road up the hill.

Architect The road up the hill.

Mother To the school.

Architect To the school. Yes.

Mother And here. Just here. Do you see?

Architect Yes. Where the road widens at the top of the rise and becomes the school car park.

Mother This is where I would have stood.

Architect Stood?

Mother Here.

Architect There.

Mother That day.

Architect I see.

Mother This is the place I stood in. You know, the number of times that I wished that I could. See. Things. Properly. Faces mainly. My baby's face. And dogs. I miss the look of dogs.

Architect Goodness.

Mother That day though. Never been so glad not to see. I made one of the boys stand behind me and tell me what was happening. 'What's happening now?' I'd say, and the boy would tell me. 'What's happening now?' Other parents arriving. 'What's happening now?' Police talking to ambulance people. 'What's happening now?' Other people, strangers, coming up the road, standing around looking at us stood like pillars. People like to look, you say.

Architect Yes.

Mother Then one of us. I don't know. It might have been me. Others have said it was me, but it sounded to me like it was coming from somewhere else. Outside of my . . . of me. But. Singing. Loud. The sound of someone singing. Then two, five, thirty. All of us from the church standing outside the school and holding hands singing. Loud. So the children would hear us, you see. In the school. We weren't sure that they would over the sound of the police on their . . . what's it? Megaphones? So we just go on singing.

And then the wind changes direction. I feel it, don't I? And there. On the wind. Up high. Coming and going. Children's voices. Singing. Singing back to us. Singing together with us. It was hard. If we sang too loud we couldn't hear them and if we sang too soft they might not hear us. But there they were. Children singing. A choir of children singing over the sound of the gunshots.

And then less children singing. Ten, twelve or so. And less. Three or four. Then. Just us. Singing.

And I stop singing and say, 'What's happening now?'

Police going in. 'What's happening now?' One of the mothers beside us being held down on the ground by her husband, not screaming, just her mouth open. 'What's happening now?' Some of the older kids who have brothers and sisters at the school are running around the place tearing clumps of their hair out. 'What's happening now?' Bags coming out. On trolleys. Little bags on trolleys pushed by policemen. Pushed from policeman to fireman to ambulance to mother. Bag after bag after bag after bag.

The Mother has her hands around the model schoolhouse.
Pause.

Architect (*soothing, gentle*) And that is why we have made you this.

Mother This?

Architect This memorial. For your children. For you.

Mother Yes?

Architect Yes.

Mother I understand.

Architect You understand.

Mother I understand now.

Architect Good. Good, I'm glad. That's really good.

The Architect steps towards the Mother.
Suddenly, the Mother prises the model schoolhouse from the model town and holds it in her hands.

Architect Wait! Be very / careful!

Mother Raze it to the ground!

Architect What?

Mother The school!

Architect What did you say?

Mother Raze it to the ground!

Architect Raze . . .?

Mother This is what I'm telling you, what I came here to tell you. This is what *she* wants, what *I* want, what you must do.

Architect I'm sorry . . . 'must do'?

Mother Listen . . . listen. / Listen to me.

Architect I'm listening.

Mother When I think of my daughter. I look up. Up to the sky. Not down. Not to this. (*The model.*) Do you understand me? Giving us this . . . this . . . That's like being handed back a . . . coffin. Open. For ever. In front of you. Do you see?

Architect Yes, I do see, but I'm afraid / this is what has been agreed upon.

Mother And it's not just her as well. It's . . . it's – When people go through something like this –

Architect Please be careful . . .

Mother – it makes belief hard. For them. Do you see what I'm saying now? Hard to go on believing in the face of this. Of something like this. So, our church. Our community. We keep losing. People. Not just our children. Now we lose the parents. They come to me and say. They say, 'How could this be possible?' They say, 'How could He have let this happen?' 'How could there be such evil in man?' 'How do we forgive this act?' You see? And then they fall away. Disappear. Lost. Lost to . . . to the comforts of belief. The ones on the . . . your project board. They say. They say, 'Let them go. People have to find their own way.' But every week more and more families leave us. I don't blame them for it. What sort of person would keep believing in the face of this?

Architect I'm not sure –

Mother And there's the older children.

Architect The older?

Mother The older ones. The brothers and sisters of the ones that died. They sit up there. All times of day and night. Sit up at the school. They wish they'd been killed too. Ashamed to still be alive. I've never heard anything like that. Children ashamed to be alive. Children shouldn't be ashamed to be alive.

Architect Absolutely. And there are people you should be talking to. Aren't there? Counselling. People. Whose job it is . . . But I'm . . . we're . . . I'm not sure what it is you're expecting us to –

Mother I've been telling you.

Architect Then I must be particularly dense, / because –

Mother Give us something!

Architect Give you?

Mother We need to see that there was meaning in it!

Architect I'm sorry. Meaning?

Mother Yes. To . . . to. I'm not making any . . . to put back . . . meaning . . . to put back belief . . . to show that even in *this*, *His* hand was present . . . that they didn't just die for nothing . . . Do you understand? . . . *This* is what I want! *This* is what my daughter wants! *This* is what we need! Give us something! Something! A statue! A tower! A . . . anything, anything! Just not this! (*The model.*)

The phone rings. The Architect answers.

Architect Hello? . . . Hello?

Dead.
The Architect checks her watch.

Look.
We really don't . . .
Can you . . . ?
Wait!

Mother What are you . . .?

Architect Just one . . .

The Architect leaves the room and almost immediately returns with an expensive-looking document.
She pulls up a chair, sits and opens the document.

I want to read you something. We don't have long. Here: 'The design must create a memorial that allows for a collective experience. It must provide a place of relative quiet for contemplation for the wider public.'

She closes the document.

There.

She looks at her watch.

Mother What is that?

Architect The brief.

Mother The . . .?

Architect The original brief. For your / memorial . . .

Mother It's not my –

Architect No mention of – and I'm sorry to have to put it like this to you, but, the clock is ticking – no mention of, as you say it, 'meaning', only 'collective experience', 'relative quiet', 'wider public'. What we've done here. In consultation with the project board. *Your* project board. Is a fitting expression of that brief. I believe. Now if you'll –

Mother It happens all the time though.

Pause.

Architect Excuse me?

Mother It happens all the time. People. Doesn't it? Don't they? Building things? To help people. Believe.

Architect I . . . I'm not sure I . . . ?

Mother All over the world. People. Building things. To help people see. Feel. God.

Architect I suppose . . .

Mother So . . . ?

Architect Well . . .

Mother I'm right. Aren't I?

Architect Once upon a time, perhaps. Once upon a time it was the architect's job to, as you say, to . . . to 'help people see. Feel'. It was one of the purposes of cathedrals, wasn't it? Wren with St Paul's. Bramante with St Peter's. Gaudi with the Sagrada. Yes?

Mother I don't –

Architect Domes. Towers. To create awe. To create, well as you say, a feeling of . . . of God. As you say; 'meaning'. Yes? You're right. You are absolutely right. But not now. Not with this. Here it's our job to. Simply to . . . to create a . . . a context. Yes? A context for people to have their *own* experience of the site. We're simply presenting people with the facts, the truth of what happened and allowing them –

Mother According to . . .

Architect I'm sorry?

Mother The truth according to . . .

Architect Well, the truth isn't according to anyone, is it? It's just the truth.

The phone rings. The Architect answers.

Hello? . . . Hello?

Dead.

The taxis are probably . . .

She runs a hand through her hair.

Please try to. You have to try and understand. You talk about. About. About looking up. To the sky. To heaven. About a statue. And I do understand. I really do. But we're attempting to make people look ahead. Dead ahead.

Mother Dead . . .?

Architect Yes. No. Look. It's like. You know what it's like? It's like a Venus flytrap.

Mother Venus?

Architect A plant. Beautiful. You know? It draws people in. Flies in. It's a type of plant that draws things into it and then closes around the thing. Insects. That sort of. And this is like that. People go to your town. Fascinated to see the thing. To see the. You've said it yourself. And yes, perhaps motivated by . . . by . . . not exactly something altruistic but by something dark, black, voyeuristic even, perhaps. But once there, the facts of that day close around them and they're trapped by their own fascination. To face the day. To face many such days the world has had. The . . . the . . . awfulness. The . . . the indiscriminateness. And . . . and they see. Don't they. No story. No . . . what is it? Narrative. Just. See. Life and . . . and yes, death. As it is. The truth.

Pause.

Mother Have you stopped?

Architect Yes. No. Just. We know it may be controversial. Brave even? But by preserving the building and not building something overtly . . . well . . . overt, like you're

suggesting, we're providing for a '*collective* experience' for the '*wider* public'. A context. Back to that brief again. Yes?
Now, if you don't mind can I have my –

Mother What about the families?

Architect The . . .?

Mother *Our* families?

Pause.

Architect Yes.
And here's where I . . .

Mother What?

Architect You say 'our families', but all I see here is one person.

Mother All you see?

Architect Yes. In front of me. All I see is . . . you.

Mother Yes.

Architect So. That raises a question for me.

Mother What question?

Architect Where are the rest of the families? The other members of your –?

Mother They. We.

Architect It's a question of authority. Really. I ask myself: 'where is your authority?' And the answer? Well . . .

Mother I. I.

Architect Yes. I hear everything that you are saying. But. I'm sorry. And with the greatest respect. It doesn't seem to me that you are speaking for your community. That you have the authority to speak for your community.

Mother They. They.

Architect You see my point then.

Mother They don't understand. They're happy with . . . with . . . with. But they don't see. They think I'm . . .

Architect Yes?

Mother Never mind.

Architect Yes.

Mother I . . .

Architect Yes?

Mother No.

Architect So. Now. If you'd just . . . Would you mind very much if I had my coat back?

Defeated, the Mother goes to take the coat off.
As she is being careful of the model something small falls with a crack from the coat pocket to the floor.

Mother What's . . .?

Architect It's . . .

Mother Your pocket. From your pocket.

The Architect goes to pick it up.
The Mother beats her to it, feeling for the thing on the ground in front of her. She locates it.
It's a small toy that might belong to a six-year-old boy.

Architect It's . . .

Mother A toy.

Architect Yes. I must have –

Mother A child's toy.

Architect Yes. Don't worry about –

Mother Your child.

Architect Ah. Yes.

Mother You have a child?

Architect Yes. I must have put that in my pocket.

Mother (*holding out the toy so the Architect can take it*) You have a child.

The Intern comes in.

Intern I was ringing.

The Architect grabs the toy.

Architect What? Yes.

Intern The taxis are here.

Architect What?

Intern The / taxis are here.

Architect Great! Good! At last! And I suppose I look – I must look a mess now. With all this. And I haven't got time. I was going to. I don't suppose you . . . ?

Intern I've got some make-up. If that's any –

Architect Perfect!

Intern If that's what you mean?

Architect Yes. That'd be great. Thanks.

Intern It's in my bag . . . I'll . . .

Architect Terrific. Thank you. Thanks.

The Intern goes.

So. We should –

Mother Where is she, then?

Architect I'm sorry?

Mother Your child. Your –

Architect Oh. *He* . . . he's with his father.

Mother And where is the mother?

Architect She's here . . . I'm . . . I'm here.

Mother Why aren't you with your child, then?

Architect Because I'm . . . as I've said, this is an extremely important / night for us.

Mother The busy mother.

Architect Yes. No. Just. The mother.

Mother Does he live with you, then?

Architect I'm sorry. With all due respect, I'm not sure that's any of your –

Mother Why doesn't he live with you, then?

Architect Because he lives with his father.

Mother Why does he live with his father?

Architect Because he does.

Mother But why?

Architect Because he does.

Mother And you live alone?

Architect Except when my son is with me. Yes.

Mother A beautiful house.

Architect I'm sorry?

Mother Your home.

Architect An apartment. Yes.

Mother With views of the river. I can see it.

Architect Can you.

Mother White. Clean.

Architect Actually, not that clean.

Mother Coming home at the end of the day with / sandwiches you got on your way –

Architect I'm going to have to ask you –

Mother – too busy to cook.

Architect I'm sorry, but this has nothing to do with –

Mother Is there something wrong with you?

Architect Excuse me?

Mother I said –

Architect I heard what you said.

Mother I just want to know what sort of person you are. That's all.

Architect Sort of . . .?

Mother I just want to know what sort of person would give us something like this.

Architect Sort of . . .? Sort of . . .? I'm. I'm a considerate. Bright. Yes, a perfectionist that sometimes makes me. Hard to be with. I am aware of that. Of how I can . . . But, I think, a loyal friend. A fair colleague. A skilful draughtsperson. A good architect. Recognised as one, at least. Recognised by others as one. Recognised by many others as one.

Mother But your son –

Architect Lives with his father. That's all. My work. My career. And we discussed. When we separated. Evenly. Properly. Dividing the practice between us both. He took the residential, which he always had a natural flair for anyway. I took the commercial. The big stuff. This. Sort of stuff. Which is my area. And it was decided, as well, that it was best for him . . . the . . . our son . . . to live with his father. His father was always good. Good with being a. So. And I travel a lot. So. We decided. Best for the child. The child should live with its father . . . his. *His!* Father.

Mother I couldn't let my daughter live with someone else.

Architect It's not someone else, it's his father.

Mother Still . . .

Architect Are you . . .? If you are trying to draw some sort of ancient line between my religious beliefs, or more correctly, my lack of them, and my abilities as a mother. The bad mother. The corporate mother. The godless mother who abandons her child. The mother who cares more for her career than for her son. The mother who is more like a man. If you are trying to make a point like that then I am afraid you are on very thin ground . . . ice . . . shaky –

Mother I'm just saying.

Architect Yes?

Mother What sort of person are you, that's all.

Architect And you? What sort of . . .? Your parenting of your daughter, then? . . .

Mother / I have no –

Architect When she was alive. What sort of parent were you? What were . . . Let me ask you a question, then. What were your hopes for your daughter then?

Mother My . . .?

Architect Yes. I'm sorry. What were your hopes?

Mother That she . . . that she . . .

Architect Is your daughter allowed to be an architect? Was. Would your daughter have been allowed to be an architect?

Mother I don't –

Architect If we're going to play . . . You say you don't want this. That. There. In your hands.

Mother She has told me –

Architect That you want something. A statue. A something. For meaning. Belief. And let's call a . . . Let's be frank here. What you're really asking for is religious. Isn't it?

Mother Yes.

Architect So. I'm assuming that your daughter shared your belief . . . your faith . . . your religious . . . practices.

Mother She did.

Architect And you were content?

Mother I don't understand you.

Architect You were content for your daughter to belong to a religious organisation –

Mother / Our faith was a real thing to her . . . not a . . . not a choice.

Architect – to have religious affiliations that said . . . that suggested that she was inherently not as important, not as significant, not as equal, not as creative, not as powerful not as . . . less . . . less than a man?

Mother Men and women have different / roles, that's all.

Architect Do they! So. Let me ask you. What would you have done?

Mother Done?

Architect Yes. Done. If she had come to you / and said –

Mother She has come to me.

Architect – 'I want to go away to university and be an architect. I want to be an architect. Mummy'?

Mother I. I . . .

Architect Thought as much.

Pause.

I'm sorry. I'm sorry, but. Please. Don't question the way. Don't question me. God. Is it hot in here? Are you hot? Is it hot?

Trying to open the window.

Can't. Get. These. To.

Mother Your son.

Architect Just a moment.

Mother Your son.

Architect Wait one –

Mother Your son.

Architect (*reeling from the window*) Alright. My son. Yes?

Mother If he died.

Architect If he died, yes?

Mother If he did. You'd want something.

Architect Yes. Something like this probably. Like that. (*The model.*) There. The truth.

Mother That word again.

Architect Which . . .?

Mother The truth.

Architect Yes.

Mother Why tell the truth with our children?

Architect Because it's the truth, not a choice.

The Intern returns with make-up.

Intern Here.

Architect Brilliant!

Intern Is everything . . .?

Architect What? Yes. It's fine.

She gives the make-up to the Architect.

Intern I'm not sure it's your –

Architect My lips are so dry from the heat. Anything would do.

She begins to put on the make-up. Perhaps she uses the window as a mirror.

What a sight.

Intern I've told them to wait.

Architect Them?

Intern Taxis.

Architect Great.

Mother Can I have some?

Architect Damn!

Intern What?

Architect / I just stabbed myself in the eye.

Mother Can I have some of that lipstick?

Intern Um. Of course you can.

Mother I haven't worn lipstick in a long time.

Intern Yes. I wouldn't have thought –

Mother My daughter loved to pretend to put make-up on. Always using crayons to put red on her cheeks and her lips. She thought I didn't know. But I knew. It must be somewhere inside them, mustn't it? Girls. Don't you think? That part of them that wants to look pretty? She didn't get it from me. Like she was putting it on to spite me. She could be like that. Spiteful. Can I . . .?

Architect Of course. Here.

Mother (*to the room*) Can you . . .?

Intern Let me . . .

She takes the lipstick and puts it on for her.

Architect Do you want me to give you a hand to get this (*the model town*) downstairs?

Intern Sorry?

Architect You're going to need a hand –

Intern That's a good colour on you. Shows off your –

Mother Is it?

Architect Yes. Yes, it is. You look pretty.

Mother Good. I'll come with you, then.

Long pause.

Intern You'll . . .?

Mother I'm coming with you.

Architect You don't understand.

Mother You'll only need one taxi. I'm a stakeholder. / One of the – I should be able to come with you to the presentation.

Architect Yes. You most certainly are, but I'm not sure that you . . .

Mother . . . I'm going to come with you. To the presentation!

Long pause.

Architect (*to Intern*) Will you just go down and let them know we're on our way?

Intern Are you sure . . . ?

Architect Please.

Mother (*holding out the lipstick, smiling*) Thank you.

Intern Why don't you keep it? (*Lipstick.*) You look good in it. A bit of colour.

Mother Thank you.

Architect The taxis . . . ?

Intern We're on our way. Yes.

Mother I'll see you downstairs.

Intern Alright.

The Intern leaves.

Mother Would you help me down please?

Architect No. I . . .

Mother What's that?

Architect You.

Pause.

I think it's time we were . . . I think it's time we were clear. Yes? Yes. I appreciate your circumstances. Empathise. You believe your daughter has come to you. Appeared to you . . . and that's . . . I don't want to go into that. It's not for me to say. Who's to say? Certainly not me. And you've come a long way. I appreciate that. But. You're not coming with us. Tonight is extremely important to us. Me. I'm sorry. I really am. It seems to me that you have an agenda which is at odds with the spirit of this monument – God! – memorial. There's no place at a function like this for agendas. For . . . well . . . / of that kind anyway.

Mother What does that . . .?

Architect It means that you need to give me back that model and take the taxi back to the train station and the train from the train station back to your home. I'm really sorry you've had to come all this way. Now if you'll just give me –

She tries to take the model from the Mother. A little tussle.

/ Please be careful!

Mother Don't! Not!

The Mother breaks away, towards the door. She still has the model.

Mother I was like you.

Architect Excuse me?

Mother Lost.

Architect I'm not –

Mother I'm not as smart as you are, though.

Architect I didn't say. / If you could hand me back the model.

Mother I'm not an *architect* or anything special like you. Just a woman. A mother. Of a dead girl. Who believes in God. It doesn't matter that that belief saved my life, does it? That I'm alive today because of it. That I could tell you a story about the person I was. The addicted person I used to be . . . the men and my father and being thrown out of home and how today I'm different because of faith. I'm a mother. *Was* a mother because of faith. I could tell you things. About what faith has done for me. But all that would make no difference to you, would it? I know you. I see you. The others don't. But I do. You come to our town now. Every weekend. Hundreds of you. To go to the school. To look at us. Like a . . . like a flytrap? 'How silly,' you think. 'How' – what is it – 'funny, old-fashioned' – what's the word – it's, it's *quaint*! 'How quaint.' Don't they know that the world is a different place now? Don't they know that there's no such thing as God now? Don't they know that the big scientists have proved that now?' 'Who'd be so stupid to believe now?' And really. Underneath. You're all thinking: 'They sort of . . . didn't they? They sort of brought this on themselves. Didn't they? Don't you think? With all this talk of God and belief. They sort of deserved it.'

Architect I have never said / anything of the kind.

Mother But you think it. You can barely cover your . . . what's the word for it? Disdain . . . isn't it?

Architect Disdain? Disdain? You want to talk about disdain? It's . . . many people would say that you are very, very lucky indeed to have us working on this site for you and not some . . . some . . . well . . . not some 'man with a plan', frankly. Our process . . .

Mother Process again.

Architect Yes, our process. Has been nuanced and respectful and democratic and, to be honest, very compassionate, I think. Very reasonably thought through. Humane. Human. And, here's the thing. For you to come here and . . . I'm sorry, but to be honest . . . to, to, to . . . demand . . . yes? I don't think that's an overstatement. To demand that we do something else. Raze the school to the ground and build something else. A statue or whatever . . . *that's* disdain. That's pretty disdainful if you ask me. Not just to me but to the project board and to our . . . yes, our process, and, frankly, to our artistry.

Mother You're an artist?

Architect I'm . . .? No. Yes. Of sorts.

Mother And you think this is art?

Architect I'm . . . I'm . . .

Mother You think this is art?

Architect No. I . . .

Mother Oh, I've just. I'm so stupid . . . I'm . . . You think . . . you think that this is art. Don't you?

The phone begins to ring.

Architect No. I.

Mother You do . . .

Architect / Please hand me back the model.

Mother Don't you? You think this is art.

Architect / Please hand me back the model.

Mother We have an artist here. An artist. Here. A . . . one of those clever, clever artists . . . / She thinks this is art . . .

Architect Some people might say –

Mother This isn't art.

Architect No. It's . . . / I have to ask you to hand me back the model. Please hand me back the model. Hand me back the model. Hand me back the model. Hand me back the model. I have to ask you to . . . ALRIGHT, ALRIGHT, ALRIGHT, ALRIGHT! IT'S NOT ART! IT'S A WARNING!

Mother How can you call this art? How can you stand there and say that this . . . this . . . *thing* is art? This . . . shell is art? How can you say that? TELL ME! You . . . you . . . *artist* . . . sitting here . . . in the city . . . sitting here and reading your newspapers and drinking your . . . your coffee and –

What?

Architect Nothing. Don't worry. It's –

Mother A WARNING OF WHAT?!

Architect RELIGION!

The phone stops ringing.

I'm sorry, I'm sorry, I'm . . . That's not what I. It's the rush. The time. The. I know we're not supposed to –

Mother (*disgust – triumph?*) So much for your process!

Architect – to . . . to . . . to have these thoughts –

Mother / So much for your . . .!

Architect – to say these things. As good people . . .

Mother / Good . . .?

Architect – as reasonable people. As human . . . humane . . . progressive . . .

Mother / What *things*? What are you talking about?

Architect . . . But I've. You ask me for meaning. *Me* of all people. To, to, to restore meaning. Faith. Isn't it. To you. With a, with a, with a . . . something. But. But. Look!

Mother / At . . . ?

Architect Look at what you're holding!

Mother What I'm / holding?

Architect Holding, yes.

Mother What are you . . . ?

Architect At what's in your hands!

Mother What?

Architect Proof!

Mother Proof?

Architect Of what I'm saying. Of what we all. Don't we?

Mother What you're . . . ?

Architect If ever we suspectected that religion was dangerous before, today we have proof. These days we have proof. These times we have. Look around. The world. Look in your hand.

Mother How is this . . . ?

Architect For God's – a . . . a . . . a man.

Mother A man?

Architect Please, please. I don't wish to be cruel, but a man.

Mother Which?

Architect Yes. A sad. Gullible. Simple? Comes to your school.

Mother No. / Please.

Architect Yes. There. That school in your hands. He wakes up one day and climbs out of bed and gets in his car and drives to a little religious school, in a pretty little town, in a green valley, in the middle of nowhere with a grievance and a gun in his pocket. To . . . to . . . to make a point . . . a point like . . . like . . . I don't know . . . like 'God is great' . . . or 'My God is right' . . . or 'Your God is wrong' . . . or 'This is how my God says you get into Paradise' . . . or 'This is what happens if you don't believe in my God' . . . or 'This is because of what your God did to me when I was seven' . . . or God only knows, and you *still* insist on –

Mother Believing! / Yes.

Architect After all this!

Mother I will always choose God over the truth!

Architect I . . . I . . . I . . . I. Yes! Yes! How. Of course. Of course. I suppose so. Except. Except this. This one thing. This. One. Truth. Your children. Your beautiful, beautiful . . . were *not* little . . . little . . . little what's the . . .? A man. As much a victim as them. A sad, sad man came into their school. That school. There. In your hands. That school in your hands. With a grievance and a gun. There is no meaning there. How could there be a meaning there?!

The phone begins to ring again.

Mother What?

Architect I have to go.

Mother What did you say?

Architect I have to go.

Mother You said he was . . .?

Architect What . . .?

Mother What did you say?

Architect When?

Mother As much a victim?

Architect I must ask you to hand / me back the model . . .

Mother As much a victim?

Architect Now, please hand me / back the model . . .

Mother As much a victim?

Architect Please hand me / back the –

Mother As much a –

Architect Yes. Yes, that's what I said. As much a victim. As them. Too. As well as. Yes.

The phone stops.
Slowly, inexorably the Mother begins to crush the model of the school.

Architect NO! WHAT ARE YOU –?!

The Architect tries to prise the crushed model from the Mother's hands.
The two women struggle with each other. Clumsy, ugly, bitter and visceral.

/ DON'T! PLEASE! STOP! STOP IT! GIVE ME. GIVE ME. YOU CAN'T JUST! JUST! STOP! STOP! STOP! STOP IT! PLEASE! JUST! STOP!

Mother A VICTIM?! THAT MAN WAS A MURDERER! YOU PEOPLE ARE ALL! THINKING THAT EVERYONE'S A VICTIM! EQUAL! IN THE WORLD! HE WAS A MURDERER!

Out of the mêlée a hand goes flying.
A crack as bone meets bone.
The Mother breaks away from the Architect.

She still has the model.

Now you can –

Architect Wait!

Mother What?

Architect You. You're bleeding.

Mother I'm . . .?

Architect Your nose.

Mother My . . .?

Architect Your nose is bleeding.

Mother It's. (*She wipes it with a sleeve.*)

Architect (*going to her*) Here.

Mother No!

Architect Your nose is bleeding, for God's sake!

Mother Stay there!

Architect Would you let me –

Mother Stay there! You . . .

Architect Please –

Mother Now you can listen to me. You with your talk. Even if it takes me a. A lifetime. I will tear down that school brick by brick. Tile by tile. Beam by beam. Tear up the carpets. Smash through the windows. Pull the blackboards from the walls. You can keep trying to – what? – preserve it? The truth? Is that right? Every scuff mark? Is that it? Like jam? You can do that. But every time, I will come back. Again and again and again. Until there is nothing. Just a rise in the middle of a town. Just a rise. No trace of –

Architect (*derisive*) Oh, for God's sake!

Mother STOP! Saying that.

Architect What?

Mother You're always saying that.

Architect What?

Mother 'For God's sake'. You're. You're always saying that. Taking the Lord's name . . . 'For God's sake', 'for God's sake', 'FOR GOD'S SAKE!' You're always –

Architect I'm . . .?

Mother Yes. Just. WILL YOU JUST STOP SAYING THAT! IT'S DISRESPECTFUL! YOU SORT OF PEOPLE ARE ALL THE SAME!

Suddenly the Architect launches herself at the Mother, pushing her to the ground.
She wrests the model from her hands and retreats back to the other side of the room.
Stunned.
At what she's done.
At what has happened.
The Mother slowly gets to her feet.

Yes.

Architect Yes.

Mother Yes, I see.

Architect Yes.

Mother Yes.

She feels for the door and makes her way out of the room.

Architect Wait! You can't . . .

She goes to the door but then thinks again and turns her attention to the destroyed model. She scans the room for implements.

The Intern is at the door with a bunch of flowers.

Intern I heard something.

Architect Here. Quickly. Get me glue, a knife.

Intern What?

Architect JUST GO!

Intern It's here. Look.

The Intern goes somewhere in the room leaving the flowers and gets the things.

The two women hover over the destroyed model.

Architect Here. Give me that. There. If we –

Intern How did this –?

Architect She attacked it. Attacked me.

Intern She? Should we? Should we call someone? / Do you think?

Architect No. We have to get going. Did you see her? / On her way out?

Intern I didn't see anyone.

Architect She . . . she got in one of the taxis.

Intern No.

Architect Yes. / She must have made it to the taxis.

Intern No. I was ringing to say. Trying to say. They left.

Pause.

Architect She's . . . She would have . . . she'll be alright. Here. Hold this. (*A piece of the model.*)

Intern Here?

Architect No. Here.

She takes the Intern's hand.

Intern You're shaking.

Architect I'm? Here.

She relinquishes the model to the Intern.

You do it. See if you can get the gable to stick.

Intern The?

Architect HERE, HERE, HERE, HERE! / See if you can do it!

Intern I can't. I don't think. Do you mean this piece / here?

Architect NO! HERE!

Intern You're scaring me.

Architect Oh, for God's sake!

Intern I'm sorry you're –

Architect Here. Give it to me. / I'll. Damn. Where's the . . .?

Intern No. Don't worry. Here. / I'll try. I'll do my best.

Architect Just, just, just. No. No. HERE!

Intern Where?

Architect Here.

Intern I don't . . .

Architect HERE, FOR GOD'S . . .!

Intern I can. I can . . .

Pause.

Architect No. It's too late.

She takes the crushed model from the Intern and puts in on the model rise.
Long pause.

The rain's stopped.

Intern Yes.

Architect I tried to open the window.

Intern Do you want me to?

Architect No. Don't worry. Will you do me a favour?

Intern I'm sure I can get it open.

Architect No. Will you . . . My hands are shaking. Will you hold them. Just. Just until they stop.

Intern Oh. Um. Yes. Alright.

The Architect, who is probably sitting down by now, offers her hands to the Intern, who puts them between her two hands.

Is that –?

Architect Yes. That's. Thank you.

Intern How did she do this?

Architect She crushed it.

Intern Awful.

Architect Yes.

Intern These people. They're . . .

Architect What?

Intern Feverish. With their . . . extreme . . . fundamental . . . No wonder . . . well . . . it's sad really.

Architect Yes.

Intern Embarrassing.

Architect Yes.

Intern No wonder you're shaking.

Architect Yes.

Intern I think it's awful.

Architect There was blood.

Intern Blood?

Architect From her nose.

Intern Surely not.

Architect Yes.

Intern How?

Architect I don't know.

Intern By rights we should call someone.

Architect By rights, yes.

Intern Should I call someone? Would you like me to do that?

Architect No. No, thank you.

Intern Your hands feel cold.

Architect Do they?

Intern They do.

Architect Do you mind if we just take a moment?

Intern No. No, not if you don't.

Long pause.

The city at night.

Pause.

I don't want to rush you . . . but –

Architect Rush me . . . ?

Intern They'll be wondering where you are.

Architect Yes. Can you . . . can you go? Why don't you go?

Intern What would I say?

Architect Tell them . . . tell them there won't be a presentation tonight.

Intern No presentation.

Architect Not tonight. No.

Intern But what if –

Architect It'll be fine. Really. Tell them there won't be a presentation tonight.

Intern Alright.

Architect Thank you.

The Architect smiles.
She stands, keeping her hands between those of the Intern, and carefully kisses her on the cheek.
The Intern starts and pulls her hands away.

Intern Should I? Should I? Should I?

Architect Thank you. You've been very helpful.

Intern I've? I'm glad. Thank you for letting me help.

She makes to go and then:

You know I was thinking . . . I'm sorry . . . It can wait.

Architect No. Go ahead.

Intern Really?

Architect Yes.

Intern It was just . . . what you said before.

Architect What I said before?

Intern About our ability to build.

Architect Oh.

Intern It's . . . while I was waiting for the taxis. Downstairs. In the dry. And watching the rain. On the black of the street. You . . . you say it makes us human . . . means we're humans.

Architect What does?

Intern Our ability to build.

Architect Um . . . yes . . . yes. I suppose. It does.

Intern It's just that . . . well . . . I'm not sure I agree.

Architect Oh.

Intern As I was standing there. In the dry. And watching the city. In the wet. I thought. I thought our ability to build is . . . it's just a more sophisticated version of the bird's ability to nest really, isn't it?

Architect Is it?

Intern We build because we need shelter, a place out of the rain, a place to be, a place for our things. Just because we may, from time to time, make something which has beautiful properties doesn't mean that it has any more merit than an ant's nest. Less actually, because so much of what we do is superfluous to need.

Architect I see.

Intern I need shelter from the rain, I build a house. I need a book, I build a library. I need to get around, I build a train station. I need to remember. I build a memorial. A building is, first and foremost, an expression of the truth of its purpose. It's the unequivocal, simple, filling of its function that makes it beautiful. Like a spoon or a cup. A building is not an idea it's a utensil. A beautiful utensil.

Architect Then what's our job, then?

Intern Our job? It's just to look. I think. To see. To see what's there. We're just. Well. Animals. That's what I was trying to say before.

Pause.

Anyway. For what it's worth. Oh. These came. (*The flowers.*)

Architect Goodness.

Intern I know. Aren't they. Do you want me to . . .?

Architect No, it's fine. Gosh. They're.

Intern Aren't they. No smell. I checked.

The Intern leaves.

The Architect takes the flowers. Looks for somewhere. Puts them in a rubbish bin.

She goes to the window and gives it one last try. Nothing.

She dials a number on her phone.

Architect It's me . . . hello . . . can you put him on? I know, but . . . can you put him on? It's . . . just . . . he won't mind . . . I know it's late . . . but . . . can you put him on? Can you put him on? Can you put him on? Can you put him on? Can you put him on? Can you . . . look . . . just . . . put him on! Can you? –

She hangs up.

A moment.

She dials the number again.

I'm sorry, I'm sorry . . . I don't mean to . . . Oh . . . alright. Well, if he's awake? Yes. Thank you.

She waits.

She clears a patch in the condensation on the window.

A young child.

A girl, wet from head to toe, is on the other side of the glass peering in.

I woke you . . . It's late for you to be awake . . . Why weren't you asleep, then? . . . What were you playing? . . . What were you drawing? . . . I'm at work . . . No. It's just me . . . Well. It's a room . . . There's a big table. With a toy town on it . . . Model town. Yes . . . that's right . . . Well, it's quite a pretty little town really . . . It's very . . . green . . . Do you? I like green too . . . There's a little library. And a road. And some shops. There's a little hill . . . No. There's no school. No . . . I don't know where the children go to school . . . Perhaps they don't. Perhaps there are no children here. I don't know. But there's no school . . . No . . . No school . . . What's that? . . . Oh . . . You don't want me to do that . . . Trust me, you don't . . . If you heard me you wouldn't be asking. I'm not very good . . . I'm just not . . . Really? . . . Alright. And then bed . . . don't say I didn't warn you . . .

Slowly, tentatively, the Architect starts to sing down the phone.

The model town glows.

The Architect and Child caught in its radiance.

End.